Advance praise for "The Hidden Profit Center"

"Investing the short time it takes to read 'The Hidden Profit Center' will pay dividends for years to come. You can't beat the ROI on this book!"—*Ian Percy, psychologist and author of 'The 11 Commandments for an Enthusiastic Team - collaborating with purpose and passion.'*

"The colourful main characters guide us to specific areas where practical and attitudinal change are the big winners for any organization. I recommend this for anyone who wants to recharge their team and challenge existing practices."—*Leah Leslie, Director of Sales & Marketing, Toronto Marriott Eaton Centre*

"I will give each one of my board members and each senior manager a copy of 'The Hidden Profit Center'. It is a great illustration of the importance of communication to the bottom line." —*Edward Barisa, CEO, Ontario Real Estate Association*

"Instead of cutting budgets, any CEO should read this book and utilize its ideas to save money. This is a hard-case scenario of how much a company can lose by not taking communication seriously."—*Peter Urs Bender, author of 'Secrets of Power Presentations' and 'Gutfeeling'.*

" 'The Hidden Profit Center' is a simple parable with a rich message for all business people. Wilkie shows the reader the hard and soft dollar cost of poor communication and how it can harm your business without your knowing. She also provides the reader with a roadmap to turn this business risk into tangible and substantial value for all stakeholders. This could easily be the best ROI available in 21st century business."—*Michael H. McInerney, CEO, The Resonance Consulting Network*

"Helen Wilkie has devised a delightful and very useful story. It should help organizations understand the urgency about clear and focused communications. In fact, she demonstrates quite easily not only the strategic advantage of good communication, but also the bottom line impact."— *Esther Ewing, The Change Alliance*

The Hidden Profit Center

A tale of profits lost and found
through communication

by
Helen Wilkie

MHW Communications
2003

National Library of Canada Cataloguing in Publication Data

Wilkie, Helen, 1943 -
      The Hidden Profit Center: a tale of profits lost and found
      through communication

ISBN 0-9684626-1-8

      1. Communication in management   I. Title

      HF5718.W528 2003   658.4'5   C2002-905453-2

Published by:
MHW Communications
90 Warren Road, Suite 202
Toronto, Ontario
Canada M4V 2S2

Cover art and book design: Felix Trindade
Editing: Vida Jurisic
Printed in Canada

To the memory of my father, Edward Wilkie, whose wonderful bedtime stories were not only a memorable part of my childhood, but the inspiration for this fable.

To my brother and sister-in-law, Bruce and Elise Wilkie, who helped me develop the story during two sunny weeks in Portugal.

And—as always—to Felix, the love of my life.

Acknowledgements

During the summer of 2002, we four sat on the beach in Costa da Caparica, Portugal—my husband Felix, my brother Bruce, my sister-in-law Elise and me. I told them my idea for a business fable illustrating the very practical importance of communication and asked if they would help me flesh out the story. When I mentioned Dad's fanciful bedtime stories, Bruce immediately saw the connection and joined in with enthusiasm. Elise and Felix were soon offering ideas too, and eventually Bruce even gave his name to one of the main characters. So huge thanks are due to these three, who helped bring the book to fruition.

My two "Butt Kickers", Lois Ferguson and Susan Birkenshaw, gave their inimitable brand of support as I tackled a very ambitious deadline. Thanks Butt Kickers!

What an advantage it is for a writer to have a good friend who is also a professional editor! Vida Jurisic made the editing process a great learning experience for me, as well as helping me convert my enthusiastic but ragged first draft into the finished book you hold in your hand. Thanks Vida!

Finally, I thank Felix also for giving shape, form and character to "Brucie", as well as designing the book and—most important of all—giving me his unfailing love and support in all that I do.

The Hidden
Profit Center

Monday night

Ten o'clock Monday night. Richard Pemberton was a worried man.

Outside his office window, the lights of a thousand tall buildings punctuated the night sky—the stone canyons of the business district never sleep. As he gazed down at a scene so familiar he hardly noticed it any more, he wondered how many offices in those other buildings contained men and women doing exactly as he was doing now—worrying.

Looking around him, he saw the trappings of success. His office, on the top floor of one of the tallest buildings in the city, was bigger than many a small apartment. Its elegant furniture and expensive art made it clearly a fitting space for the leader of a successful corporation. The discreet matte-finished brass plate on his door read, "Richard Pemberton, President and Chief Executive Officer".

He had done a good job since taking office two years ago. The company's reputation in its field was well established, and under his leadership it had grown on the strength of several new and innovative product lines. The financial picture over the past two years had looked rosy, and all three groups of stakeholders—shareholders, clients and employees—had reason to be pleased.

But now that picture was a little shaky. Sudden and rapid changes in the economic climate had affected his company as they had many others. Substantial cost savings were essential, and everyone was pushing for large staff cuts. Everyone, that is, except the CEO.

Richard hated the idea that good people had to be victims of what he devoutly hoped and believed was a temporary dip in the company's fortunes. They had worked hard and contributed to its success, and he felt certain they would be needed again when business picked up. But in the meantime, they would suffer, and he didn't want to be the instrument of their misfortune. What he needed was an alternative—another way of cutting costs drastically.

With his brain churning as it had done for hours, he hardly noticed the soft knock on the door and the quiet entrance of the cleaning lady. She pushed into his consciousness, though, when she walked straight across the wide expanse of expensive carpet to his desk, carrying her bucket and mop carefully and clutching a feather duster under her arm. Laying down her cleaning accoutrements, she stretched out her hand and introduced herself! "Hello, I'm Annie."

Startled by this unusual turn of events, Richard instinctively responded, "Hello Annie. I'm Richard. Aren't you a little late this evening? I don't usually see anyone when I stay this late."

"Oh no," said Annie, smiling, "this is just about the time I'm usually most needed." Puzzled by her reply, but too polite to ask what she meant, Richard said nothing.

Hoping to discourage further conversation, he looked down at the papers in front of him and frowned as the numbers told the same old story. But Annie was not to be easily dismissed. "Yes," she said, "it's usually about this time that they have worried so much they don't know where to go from here."

Intrigued in spite of himself, Richard asked, "Who do you mean by 'they'?"

"Oh, Presidents and other top folks. There are only so many ways you can look at a problem after all, and if they haven't come up with an answer by this time they are usually pretty worried. I can see you are."

"I can't deny that, Annie," said Richard, wondering as he said it why he didn't just ignore the woman and hope she would leave him alone. Annie smiled in a knowing way, and he had the uneasy feeling she knew exactly what he was thinking.

"Why don't you tell me what's on your mind?" she invited. While he couldn't help thinking how ridiculous this was—sitting here discussing business with the cleaning lady—something in her expression made it feel quite natural. Before he knew it, he was telling her all about the company's setback and the resulting financial dilemma. As he talked about his reluctance to fire any of his employees, his sincerity was unmistakable. He talked of his strong desire to find an alternative way of substantially reducing costs so that none of his people would find themselves jobless.

"If I fire all these people it will disrupt their lives and hurt their families," said Richard with a frown, "and it's not even a good business decision. For one thing, we will need people again later because I know business will come back up—and the good people will already have been lost to another company—but we won't even realize a true saving because it costs money to fire people. By the time we pay mandatory legal costs, as well as severance to those with contracts, we would still be far below what we need to save. Not only that, but it's just a one-time saving—what happens if we take some time to recover? We can't fire everybody!"

Annie had listened in silence as he put his troubled thoughts into words. Now she surprised him once again.

"Please listen carefully and, just for a short time, try to suspend your disbelief," she announced. "I may look like a regular cleaning lady, but I'm really something quite different. Instead of cleaning up offices, I help clean up problems for deserving people like you. Will you trust me?"

Richard couldn't understand why he was going along with this, but something in Annie's eyes compelled him to take her seriously. He found himself agreeing to trust her.

"Switch on your computer," commanded Annie. Instead of its usual start-up routine, his up-to-the-minute 23-inch flat monitor gradually came to life and a picture swam into focus. Richard recognized one of the meeting rooms just down the hall from his office. Before his bewildered eyes, the door opened and in came Dave Brighton, his Vice-President of Corporate Development, followed by Janice, his assistant. As Janice began to put coffee and donuts out on the table, Dave's direct reports wandered in, as well as a number of more junior members of the department. "I recognize this," cried Richard in amazement. "These people are there for the weekly update meeting on our new Internet marketing subsidiary. But that meeting surely took place earlier today—I think they usually meet on Monday mornings."

Instead of answering, Annie reached out and took his hand. Without understanding why—heck, without understanding any of this!—he stood up and followed as she approached the computer. She lightly touched the screen with her feather duster.

Immediately a buzzing began in his head, followed by a burst of bright light, and he felt himself drawn forward by an irresistible force—right into the computer screen! A split second later, the stunned CEO found himself standing with Annie in the meeting room, by the side of the door, watching everyone take their places.

Sensing his alarm, and recognizing it from previous

experience, Annie released his hand and said, "Don't worry. They can't see or hear us, but we will be able to watch and listen to the whole proceeding. I think you'll be surprised at what you learn."

Still Monday night

The clock on the wall told Richard that, against all logic, it was 9.30 a.m. People ambled into place, dropping into chairs and sprawling around the conference table. Desultory conversations began.

"Wasn't the traffic horrendous this morning?"

"Did you see the game last night? What a drag!"

"Oh, not these terrible donuts again! Why can't we have some of those healthy muffins from the place on the corner?"

"We tried that and nobody liked them, so we're going back to donuts."

"Where's Bob?" Dave cut in. "He's supposed to update us on the software beta testing this morning. Janice, did he confirm he would be here?"

"Well, I sent him the notice and he didn't say he wasn't coming." Ten minutes later, still no Bob—Janice called him. Eyes rolling toward the ceiling, Janice reported that Bob hadn't checked his e-mail, just got the notice now and wasn't quite ready with his report. However, he would be there in a few minutes and would give them the "quick version".

When Janice subtly pointed at her watch, Dave cleared his throat and began to speak.

"Well, OK, I guess we should get started. The purpose of our meeting is—ah—well you know, our usual Monday meeting. We'll begin with our regular reports from Marketing, Finance, Engineering and Human Resources. Let's leave the technical stuff until Bob gets here. George, why don't you start?"

George Patterson, Director of Marketing, shuffled the small pile of papers in front of him, gazed momentarily at the ceiling, then spoke. "Well, I'll just recap where we were last week." He proceeded to do so at length, concluding, "You've all had a week to study the Marketing Plan. Any comments?"

After a few moments of blank stares, a junior team member spoke up. "I don't think I got it, George. Do you have any extras?" After more shuffling, George handed over a half-inch-thick bound document. Since no other comments appeared forthcoming, George resumed. For the next twenty minutes, he went over material that sounded strangely familiar—not surprisingly, as it had already been discussed the previous week. To the relief of all, he finally finished. "Well, that's it. Nothing really new this week. I hope to have more for our next meeting."

Dave's cell phone rang. "Oops," he said, "I meant to shut this off in case we were interrupted, but I'd better just take it." During Dave's ten-minute conversation, a lively discussion of the previous night's baseball game took place around the table.

A loud knock on the door heralded the arrival of Bob Marsden, carrying a thick sheaf of papers. "Oh good, Bob's here," said Dave, quickly hanging up. "Let's just jump to his report and find out what the techies have been up to."

With no formal report to distribute, Bob summarized and explained and rambled for half an hour to an audience clearly not much wiser at the end.

Watching invisibly from the sidelines, Richard looked at Annie in disbelief. He was just as baffled as everyone else!

Several people asked questions in an attempt to understand. Unfortunately, Bob seemed incapable of saying anything without using technical jargon, and often his explanations created more confusion than clarity. Nonetheless, after forty minutes, Dave thanked him profusely for his contribution and invited him to stay for the rest of the meeting if he wished. "Might as well," replied Bob, "nothing much happening over my way today—and you folks have good donuts!"

Next came Marius Grant, Director of Finance. As he began his report, a side conversation started between Sheila Jones and Bert Saltzman. It began as a low murmur and grew in both volume and intensity as the discussion escalated into an argument. Others around the table were clearly uncomfortable, as Marius struggled valiantly to be heard. They looked from the arguing pair to the speaker to the meeting leader, eyes rolling upwards in annoyance. Finally, with no lead from Dave, Marius himself turned to the pair and said, "Sheila, Bert, is there something I am saying on which you have a comment? If you'd like to share it with the rest of us, I'd be happy to relinquish the floor."

Sheepishly, Bert admitted that a point from the previous technical report was still a bone of contention between them. Clarification from Bob revealed they were both wrong. The argument ended and Marius finished his report.

As the other regular reports were delivered relentlessly, time rolled on and Dave suddenly realized it was 11.45 a.m. "Well," he said to ten sets of glazed-over eyes, "it's almost lunchtime. We still have quite a lot to cover, so perhaps we should order in. What do you all think?" After much discussion, Janice was dispatched to place the lunch order.

"Oh, I'm sorry Dave," interrupted Deborah Swanson, an invited guest from the Promotions Department, "but I'm afraid I must leave. I was under the impression the meeting would last only the morning and I have other commitments for the afternoon."

Since Deborah's input was key to the long-awaited discussion on the launch of the new subsidiary, it was agreed that this would be postponed until the next meeting and Deborah took her leave.

The meeting dragged on and on, finally ending at three-thirty, and Richard felt truly depressed.

A loud throat-clearing "ahem" made him turn—his eyes popped and his jaw dropped. Seated at the end of the table was a five-foot white rabbit wearing bright red gloves! His long ears stood straight up, and his left eyebrow cocked upwards quizzically. This was one cool bunny!

On the table in front of him stood a large, old-fashioned

cash register—the kind that used to be in little stores selling everything from soup to nuts, before the computer chip changed everything. The kind that rang up the groceries with a loud "Ca-ching!"

Richard gaped. The rabbit spoke. "Don't look at me like that. Haven't you ever seen a rabbit before? My name is Brucie and I'm about to tally the cost of this waste of time your people call a meeting." His red-gloved paws flew over the keyboard and a paper strip snaked out of the machine as he rang up the items one by one.

"Ten regular participants and two visitors, total annual salary $1,425,000. Hourly costs for those direct salaries using the standard formula, $712.50. Multiply by the six l-o-o-o-n-g hours the meeting took. Total direct salary costs of the meeting..." Brucie's right ear suddenly bowed forward at right angles to his face, a loud "Ca-ching!" erupted from the cash register and, ripping the tape off with a flourish, Brucie read,

"Four thousand, two hundred and seventy five dollars.

"The four Directors each spent an average of ninety minutes preparing their reports. Total hourly salary $355 for all four, times six hours..." Down came Brucie's right ear, "Ca-ching!" shouted the cash register. "...two thousand, one hundred and thirty dollars!

"Typing, copying and binding the reports, four administrative assistants, total hourly salary $76, three hours." "Ca-ching!" "Two hundred and twenty-eight dollars."

Mesmerized by Brucie's bowing right ear and the "Ca-ching!" of the cash register, Richard's shocked mind took in the numbers. But Brucie wasn't finished.

"Outside printing of the four reports (the Printing Department couldn't get them done on time), ten copies plus three extras just in case." "Ca-ching!" One hundred and forty-three dollars."

"Coffee and donuts for ten people." Down came the ear. "Ca-ching!" "That's another fifty-five dollars—the cheapest item in the meeting and the first thing to go when cost-cutting comes up at budget time!" added Brucie with a knowing grin.

"Unbudgeted lunch costs..." "Ca-ching!" "One hundred and fifty dollars."

Brucie ripped the tape off the cash register, both ears bowed in concert and the machine erupted again with an extra loud "Ca-ching!". Looking at Richard with one eyebrow cocked, he announced, "This poor excuse for a business meeting cost your company a total of six thousand, nine hundred and eight-one dollars!"

With that, Brucie grinned broadly and—before Richard's astonished eyes—both he and the cash register vanished.

Annie smiled at Richard reassuringly, took his hand, twirled her feather duster in the air and before he could think any further, they were both back at his desk. The view from the window told him it was still night, and the clock confirmed they had been away only moments. Richard shook his head in an effort to regain his sense of reality.

Annie, it seemed, had settled in and was ready for a discussion. "Well," she said expectantly, "what's your reaction to what you saw and heard?"

"Not good," Richard grimaced. "If that's an example of what goes on at meetings across the company, no wonder so many projects get bogged down."

"What do you think went wrong?" asked Annie.

"Where would you like me to begin?" replied Richard ruefully. "First there was Dave's opening statement. If a person can't find a better reason to meet than just 'our usual Monday meeting', you have to wonder how effective the meeting will turn out to be. And those regular reports! George didn't need to report at all. He had nothing new to say—why didn't he just say so?"

"People are often reluctant to say that though," said Annie. "They feel that people will think they are not doing their jobs."

"And that rambling dissertation of Bob's! I had no idea what he was saying. He certainly seemed enthusiastic about the testing, but I don't think anyone else understood. I looked around afterwards and the only response was relief that it was over!

"The most important item that should have been discussed was the promotional program, which they didn't get to because the meeting took so long they lost Deborah! I can't believe it." Richard shook his head angrily.

After a moment's silence, he suddenly looked up at Annie and exclaimed, "And I had never realized the size of the price tag! $6,981 for one meeting! These people do this every week, so that adds up to nearly three hundred and fifty-thousand dollars in a year."

"And how many other meetings would you estimate take place throughout the company every day?"

"Well I know that whenever I try to reach anyone by phone, an awful lot of them seem to be constantly in meetings! There must be at least ten meetings of different sizes and lengths every day, just in this office alone—and that might be a conservative estimate. Then there are all the meetings held throughout the divisions—it just doesn't bear thinking about.

"But Annie, people do need to get together—some things *need* face-to-face discussion. So we have to meet. We can't do without meetings! "

"Certainly not," Annie replied. "It's not a matter of cutting out meetings, but of making them effective business tools. This is a communication issue, Richard. The skills involved in running a meeting—and even in taking part in other people's meetings—are communication skills, and this is just one example of how poor communication can cost your organization a lot of money. People often pay lip service to the need for good communication, but when it comes right down to it they don't see it as vital. More often it's seen as a warm and fuzzy kind of "nice to have". But what you saw tonight should prove to you that it's much more than that. Communication has a direct effect on profitability!"

"Yes, you're right, Annie. But what can I do about it?"

"The trouble is," continued Annie, "that people are just expected to somehow know these things. But how can they know if nobody teaches them? Even though survey after survey tells us communication skills are vital for effective business leaders, how much time goes into teaching these skills at business schools? Did anyone teach you how to run a meeting?"

"No. Come to think of it, nobody did," replied Richard thoughtfully. "I'll bet there's nothing about this in our training or professional development program. Maybe there should be."

"You're on the right track, Richard. Training is the key, but it needs to be the right kind of training. When you ask people to change, it's always a good idea to tell them why. It seems to me you need to show your people how they could save the company large amounts of money by improving their meetings, and *then* give them the right training to help them do that."

Richard was thoughtful. He could already see the potential savings from improving the whole meetings scenario throughout the company.

As if reading his mind, Annie said, "Yes, but didn't you just agree to slash the training budget and stop all new training initiatives until further notice, in an attempt to save money?"

With that, she stood and gathered her mop and pail,

preparing to leave. "Would you like more food for thought?" she asked with a smile. Poor Richard! He really didn't want to hear any more. But knew he needed it, so he nodded his head.

"Think about all this in the meantime, and be here tomorrow night at the same time." And she left, closing the door softly on a bewildered Richard.

Tuesday night

At ten o'clock on Tuesday night, Richard sat at his desk grappling with mixed feelings. On one hand, he was still baffled by what had happened the previous night and still his mind wouldn't completely accept that it wasn't some kind of dream. On the other hand, though, whatever had happened, he had been given insights into one very expensive problem his company faced.

Today he had attended one meeting, invited by another of his vice-presidents, and had difficulty concentrating on the substance because he couldn't help noticing similarities to what he had seen at Dave's meeting. Looking round the table, he mentally tallied the annual salaries of attendees, including his own—particularly his own, in fact, because when it came right down to it there was really no need for his presence. Although this meeting was much shorter than Dave's, he eventually costed it out at about $2,800. This meeting also failed to meet its objective and another had to be scheduled for the following week.

As an experiment, he had called managers in various divisions—60% were in meetings! How much was all this costing the company? Not easy to find out, as there was no single line on the financial statement for meetings.

So, here he sat, waiting for who knows what? Would Annie really come back, and what else would she show him?

A knock on the door brought the answer. Annie walked up to his desk, again carrying duster, bucket and mop.

"Well, Richard," she asked with a knowing smile, "have you had an interesting day?" He responded by telling her about the meeting he attended, as well as the calls to managers, then asked what she had for him tonight.

In answer, Annie raised her feather duster and pointed at the computer, already booted up on Richard's desk. The screen-saver faded away, and in its place Richard saw a scene he didn't recognize. Again with the soft touch of the duster on the screen, the buzzing began in his head, followed by the burst of bright light and the invisible force drawing him into the screen.

He and Annie stood at the back of a large conference room. About fifty men and women sat at tables arranged in a U-shape, facing a large screen. The logo currently projected on the screen told him this was a franchisee meeting of Acme

Accounting Services, a large organization that had been targeted as a potential client for his company's software. Immediately he remembered everyone's delight when Acme had agreed to have a senior sales representative address this conference. What an opportunity! If Acme's franchisees could be persuaded to introduce the software into their operations, it could represent an initial sale of about two million dollars, with ongoing income from service contracts and software updates.

Acme's vice-president of marketing was speaking.

"Folks, it's my pleasure to introduce to you Bill Moffat of Bolid Software. They claim to have some revolutionary new software products and Bill is here to tell us about them. Over to you, Bill."

As Bill walked over to the lectern with a smile, Richard waited eagerly for this presentation that could mean so much to his company.

"Uh, thanks, ah, Marty, for inviting me here today,"

said Bill, looking not at the audience but at the keyboard of his laptop computer. He was trying to find the right key to start the multi-media presentation that would wow these potential clients. The pause that followed was long enough for several side conversations to begin at the tables, but eventually the screen sprang to life with bright pictures and upbeat music. Unfortunately, Bill had to stop it immediately in order to introduce the movie!

"We are very excited about this new software," he began in a monotone that belied his words, "and I'm sure that when you have seen our multi-media presentation you will be too. I'll just let it run first to give you an idea and then I'll give you some of the detailed specs. OK?"

The Promotions Department had done a splendid job with the presentation. It positioned the company as a dynamic, cutting edge provider of business solutions, and set the stage for an informative presentation on the new software. That was to be Bill's job.

After more fumbling at the keyboard, Bill distractedly told the audience, "I'll just show you some of the features of our stuff, if I can just get this started." Finally, he did start the program. It turned out to be a long series of slides, each depicting a catalogue-style illustration and description of the entire product line.

Although the software really was revolutionary, and had clear benefits to the people in the room, Bill simply focused on what the products could do. No vivid word pictures grabbed the audience's imagination; no stories of other users made the products come alive; no connection was made between the products and their needs. Instead, after a forced march through 27 slides, Bill concluded with, "Well, that's about it. Does anyone have any questions?"

Richard had questions! He wanted to shout, "Why did you come to speak to these potentially huge clients so obviously unprepared? Why didn't you talk their language?

Why didn't you get them excited about how we could help them do better business?"

But of course, he couldn't be seen or heard. After one or two polite questions and ineffective answers, the host thanked Bill for his participation and he left. The brief discussion that followed his departure confirmed Richard's worst fears.

"Well, what do you all think?" asked the vice-president. There was head nodding and general agreement with the person who replied, "I didn't really understand most of it, but it seems to me there isn't anything very special about it or different from what we have already."

"Well, anyway, if any of you would like to contact him, his card is up here at the front. Now, on to the next item on our agenda, which I know you are all going to enjoy."

His voice faded as if someone had turned down an invisible volume knob. Suddenly Brucie appeared at the end of the table with his big cash register.

"Oops!" he said to Richard, "looks like you blew this one." Once again the red-gloved paws raced over the keys and the tally paper told its sad tale. "Value of initial sale to the company for use in all franchise offices, $2.9 million. Potential for service contracts and software updates over the next five years, $7.3 million. Total loss from this blown opportunity...". Once again, Brucie's right ear bowed in sync with the cash register's loud "Ca-ching!".

"Eleven point two million dollars!" announced Brucie—and he instantly vanished.

Richard groaned and closed his eyes. When he opened them a moment later, Annie had performed her duster-twirling act and they had both returned to Richard's office just like the night before.

"First thing in the morning I'll have to pay a visit to Joe

Mendoza, our Director of Sales. I don't know what it is, but there has to be something we can do to save this situation before the door is closed completely." Although he spoke almost to himself, Annie's reply made him look at her with apprehension.

"Well you'd better move fast, because Bill apparently thought the presentation went very well! You heard for yourself what the Acme people thought.

"But this has been an even more costly week than you realize," she continued. "Your company lost two more potential sales for the same reason. The salespeople were so keen to talk about the product that they didn't ask for, or listen to, the client's needs. That's like a doctor prescribing an operation before diagnosing the illness!"

"But I thought our salespeople knew better than that!" cried Richard. "We hire good people and I thought we were giving them good training."

"Yes, Richard, your company does train its salespeople, but you don't give enough importance to communication—and you're not alone. Most organizations make the same mistake.

"Salespeople will happily tell you it's important to sell benefits, not features. But as you saw, they often don't follow their own advice! Even seasoned salespeople see a sales presentation as a one-way process. But if nobody receives the message—where's the communication?

"In his presentation to Acme, Bill talked endlessly about the technical features of the software, and because he wasn't 'listening' to the body language of his audience, he didn't notice they had lost interest."

"So what should we do about it? I guess we need to do more training."

"Well, not necessarily *more* training, but training with a different emphasis. First you have to show your sales force how their performance is costing the company sales, then give them communication training with teeth!"

As Richard nodded thoughtfully, Annie stood up and prepared to leave. Before she opened the door, however, she turned back and said, "Oh, but didn't you just cut your training budget?"

And then she was gone.

Wednesday night

She hadn't said she would come back. As he sat before his computer just before ten o'clock, Richard was a worried, but thoughtful, man. He hoped Annie would return but worried about the bad news she might have for him tonight.

She was right on time! "I see you are ready for me," she smiled. "So what are the chances of rescuing the Acme project?"

"Well," Richard replied, "I had a heart-to-heart talk with Joe about our sales presentations. Mind you, he did wonder how I knew about the situation—it wasn't easy glossing over that one!" He smiled, remembering Joe's puzzled questions.

"First he'll go to work on Acme, and then we will tackle the communication problems sabotaging our selling process. But I've been wondering whether you would be here tonight."

Annie smiled. "Oh yes," she replied, "If you are willing, I will have something for you every night this week."

Richard needed no coaching this time, since he already knew the routine. He reached for Annie's hand, and together they once more went through the mind-boggling into-the-computer process. Blinking his eyes to recover from the bright light, Richard saw a place he recognized but rarely visited—the Accounting Department. A large, busy main floor was divided into modern open-concept workstations separated by floor dividers. Most were occupied by individuals or pairs of people equipped with the usual computer paraphernalia and other technological wizardry.

At one of these workstations sat a young woman, gazing at her computer screen intently and intermittently tapping out words on her keyboard. "Let's see what she is doing," suggested Annie.

She and Richard stood behind the woman, whose nameplate identified her as Yvonne Raleigh. Apparently, Yvonne had just started writing a report to the Director of Finance. It began,

> *You have asked me to look into how we are utilizing our own proprietary software within the Accounting Department. The reason for this investigation is to study how we can make more effective use of our own technology. In carrying out this investigation I have, as you suggested,...*

Having reached this point, Yvonne appeared to be stuck. She sat staring at her words for some time. "Let's leave her here for a while, Richard," said Annie. "I want you to see some other examples of the written communication challenges at your company." So saying, she gave a twirl of her duster and Richard felt himself sucked upwards very quickly, and just as abruptly dropped down again in another office. Although the setting wasn't familiar, he did recognize the man standing by his desk reading from a sheaf of papers. His name was Paul Martino, and his company had done business with Richard's company, Bolid Software, for several years. He was frowning.

Invisible behind his shoulder, Richard saw he was holding a service contract and reading a letter on Bolid's letterhead. Quickly, Richard scanned the letter.

> *Enclosed is your service contract renewal documentation.*
>
> *You will see the fee has been increased by 9.8%, which*

is the result of rising labour costs and travel expenses. We trust you will understand.

Please read the contract carefully to ensure it meets your needs. If so, kindly sign and return it to us within ten days of the above date in order to avoid loss of service.

We trust the above is satisfactory and look forward to continuing to be of service to you.

The letter was signed, "John Bothwell, Customer Service Representative". As Richard finished reading the letter, Paul threw it on his desk with an impatient gesture, muttering to himself.

"Service Representative! Hah! What a nerve—some service! They expect me to wade through all the 'legalese' in their contract, with nothing in the letter to help me know what to look for except they've raised their fee by nearly ten percent! That's a lot of money over the course of the contract. I don't think they've been out here more than twice in the past year, so *we* sure haven't added to travel costs. Why should we have to pay for their labour and travel costs anyway? They sure don't care much about their long-time customers."

He sat down, leaned far back in his chair and looked at the ceiling, deep in thought. Then he picked up the phone and dialled. After a few moments, he spoke to someone on the other end. "Patricia," he said, "you know that service contract we have with Bolid? Do we really need it? I mean, if anything goes wrong with the software, do you think we can take care of it in house?" After listening to Patricia's reply, he thanked her and hung up.

He dashed off a quick handwritten note to his administrative assistant telling her to write Bolid Software saying they didn't want to renew the service contract, clipped it to the letter and put it on one side. On to something else.

Before Richard had a chance to react, a flash of light

brought Brucie into view at the side of Paul's desk. "One lost service contract, total amount over the next two years..." Down came the ear, "Ca-ching!" went the cash register, "...twenty-five thousand dollars!" Brucie exclaimed—and vanished.

With a twirl of Annie's duster, they were back with Yvonne.

She chewed the end of her pen and frowned as she peered at her screen, rereading the introduction to her report.

Introduction

A need has been identified to discover how much and how effectively we are utilizing our own software products in the Accounting Department. The reason for this is to find out if we can offer our 'best practices' to our clients.

Methodology

In carrying out this investigation I have, as you

*suggested, begun by surveying everyone in Accounting.
I prepared a special questionnaire (see Appendix 1) to
find out this information......*

Richard turned to Annie in dismay. "How long has she
been working on this?" she asked. Annie replied that so far
Yvonne's report had consumed forty-five minutes of her time.
Richard shook his head. "Well," he muttered, "so far she's
used up forty-five minutes and half a page telling Marius what
he already knows. I hope things improve soon."

"Come along, Richard", replied Annie, "I've more to
show you."

Another twirl of the duster took Richard and Annie to
Human Resources, where Marcia Brown was reading her e-
mail. Seeing her puzzled expression, Richard looked over her
shoulder and read:

*About that meeting. Can we switch it back a day?
Something came up for me. Let me know.*

Tom

Marcia muttered to herself as she scanned her e-mail messages. She fired off a response:

What meeting, Tom?

Marcia

After a few moments, in came Tom's reply:

The group meeting to plan the pitch to Robb Motor Vehicles. Can you make it the day before? I don't know yet about the others.

Frustrated, Marcia called Tom. It turned out that Marcia wasn't involved in the meeting but had received the message simply because she was on one of Tom's e-mail distribution lists. As she put down her phone she didn't know whether to feel more annoyed at this waste of her time—or relieved that she didn't have to attend one more meeting!

A loud "Ca-ching!" announced Brucie's arrival. "Ten minutes of Marcia's time, totally wasted because she shouldn't even have received the message. Add twenty minutes for five others on the list—they didn't need the information either." Down came the ear, "Ca-ching!" went the cash register, "Total just $83 this time. But this scene is taking place all across the company even as we speak. Last year alone, this waste cost Bolid Software around $1 million."

"No!" cried Richard. "Surely not! I know it's a waste, but you must be exaggerating."

Brucie looked indignant. "Certainly not!" he responded. "If it's any comfort to you, your company isn't alone. Across the country it's about a $50 billion problem—$1 million is just your share of it."

The duster twirled, and as Richard found himself back with Yvonne, he saw Brucie perched on a spare desk, his trusty cash register balanced on his knee.

"This is a complicated one," he began. "First, it took Marcia nearly two hours to finish her first draft. As soon as she printed it, she began working on it again, wordsmithing and moving things around. After another hour, she printed the second draft. Realizing she did have other things to attend to, she put the draft away until next day, when she spent another ninety minutes 'perfecting' it.

"Since Marcia wanted to make a good impression on the Director, she decided to enlist the help of her colleague, Jonathan. After spending an hour picking it apart, he returned it with his comments. Marcia considered all the points carefully, rejected most of them and then spent half an hour making a few minor changes of her own.

"Unfortunately, Marius had trouble wading through Marcia's cumbersome verbiage and didn't really understand what she was recommending. So he called Marcia to his office, where they spent another hour going over the report.

"Four hours for Marcia and one hour each for Jonathan and Marius. Total cost of the report..." As Brucie's ear bowed low, the cash register fairly jumped in the air, so loud was its enthusiastic "Ca-ching!"

"...three hundred and thirty-two dollars and fifty cents!" As usual, he was gone in a flash, and in the same instant Richard was back in his office with Annie.

"So, ready for Annie's analysis?" she asked with a smile. Richard's groan said he had already done some analyzing of his own, but he told Annie to let him have it.

"Richard, people who work in offices write constantly as part of their jobs. Most don't enjoy it, think of it as a necessary evil and either rush through it as quickly as possible or, like Yvonne, spend inordinate amounts of time trying to get it right.

"Just in these few examples we saw tonight, poor writing cost Bolid over twenty-five thousand dollars. Now admittedly, most poor letters don't lead to contract cancellations—although that happens more often than you might think.

"However, studies show that writing an ordinary business memo costs an average of $83—and you can only imagine how many memos your people write every day. The advent of e-mail has only made matters worse. For some reason people think they don't have to pay as much attention to their writing as they would when writing a paper-based message. This leads to misunderstandings and wasted time, not to mention frayed tempers and ill will."

"But surely you're not suggesting we stop writing!" exclaimed Richard. "Of course not," replied Annie. "Just like meetings, written messages are necessary. But again like meetings, they need to be effective. They need to do their job, which is to communicate—not to impress a boss or anything else.

"People think they *should* know how to write, even though they have had no real training in business writing.

Again, you need to offer them a very specific type of training that first demonstrates how written communication affects profitability. Salespeople, for example, need to see their correspondence with prospects as an integral part of the sales process. Customer service people need to understand that the words and phrases they use can make the difference between happy clients and frustrated ones who will take their business somewhere else."

"I guess we're back to that training budget again, aren't we?" said Richard, knowing the answer already. He was deep in thought as Annie took her bucket and mop, and quietly left.

Thursday night

Richard tapped his fingers impatiently as he waited for Annie. Even though the lessons were tough, his sharp mind was already figuring out how to tap the Hidden Profit Center Annie's magic had shown him.

When she arrived, at ten o'clock on the dot, Richard hardly waited for her to put down her bucket before reaching for her hand. But this was Annie's show; she was the director, and she wasn't to be rushed.

"Not yet, Richard," she admonished him. "Be patient. Tonight's voyage of discovery is a little different. This time I want to show you the cost of lost opportunities. First, a question."

Deflated, Richard sank back in his chair, scowling a little.

"How much does your company spend each year on club memberships, conference and tradeshow attendance, sponsored luncheons etc. for executives, managers and employees?"

Quickly pressing a few keys, Richard brought financial reports up on his screen. After a few moments, he answered Annie's question. "Well, according to these projections, we are planning on $1,250,000 for this year."

"That's a lot of money," commented Annie. "Why do you spend so much on these items?"

"Well it may seem like a lot, but it's not out of line with industry standards. We all do this, for a couple of reasons. First, it's a perk. People at various levels in the company expect little extras on top of their base compensation and we are happy to provide them. Of course, the advantage is that we can write the expense off." Richard's explanation was given with a slightly disparaging smile at Annie, who he felt couldn't, after all, be expected to fully comprehend business details.

"Oh yes, I understand that," replied Annie, "and of course your company does benefit from spending this money. But you know, it's still an expense, and a large one."

"Well, Annie," replied Richard a little patronizingly, "if you're thinking of cutting these out of the budget, it wouldn't be enough to make the difference we need."

Annie shook her head. "No, Richard. You don't have to cut out the perks. But you *can* capitalize on the Hidden Profit Center they contain. Those who receive the perks need to learn to exploit them on behalf of the company."

Annie flicked her duster at the screen, the financials vanished and another picture appeared.

This time the location seemed to be a large ballroom laid out with round tables. Some were already full, others awaited their occupants. Hundreds of people in business clothes milled around in ones and twos, carrying food and drink, making contact with each other and moving towards tables. The buzz of conversation all but drowned out the music playing in the background.

Richard and Annie moved effortlessly through the crowd, until they came upon two faces Richard recognized.

Don Daniels and Barb Marino stood near the door, carefully balancing plates of food, glasses of wine and folders of papers as they glanced around the room. As mid-level Managers, Don and Barb owed their membership in the Chamber of Commerce to the company. They attended the monthly networking meetings, played a few rounds of golf when the opportunity presented itself and occasionally entertained friends in the Chamber's private dining room. They liked knowing they belonged, and felt it gave them a certain status among their friends and colleagues.

Today they were attending the Annual Business Awards Luncheon, a popular event that drew a wide audience of members, friends and representatives of a broad range of companies and organizations. Collectively, the attendees represented purchasing power of several million dollars.

"Where shall we sit?" asked Barb. "What about over there at that table near the platform?"

"Oh no," replied Bob. "I don't know anybody there, do you? Do you see anybody we know?"

They both looked around for a few moments and, seeing nobody they knew, decided to sit together at a table almost hidden behind a potted palm. With a bit of luck, nobody would notice that table.

A few moments later, however, they discovered they were wrong as several people drifted over and joined them. Finally seeing another colleague, Barb jumped to her feet. She waved as she called out, "Michael! Over here, Michael!"—and Michael took his place beside Don, in the last seat at their table. At this table for ten, three were from Bolid Software.

On Barb's left, a pleasant man in his thirties introduced himself. He asked a few tentative questions in an attempt to draw Barb into conversation, but her answers were less than encouraging and he eventually turned to his neighbour on the other side.

Barb now turned back to Don and Michael, and the three happily settled into conversation about familiar subjects and people.

Richard was puzzled. The other scenes Annie had shown him illustrated obvious communication blunders that were costing his company hard dollars, but he couldn't see any such mistakes here. As he pondered the possibilities, once again the volume was muted and Brucie materialized, complete with cash register, between the oblivious Don and Barb.

"That guy who tried so hard to have a conversation with Barb is Matt Hudson. He's the Vice-President of Information Systems for a multi-franchise printshop company, currently in the market for a special custom-designed software package for its new computer infrastructure. If Barb had made the effort, she might have found that out, and it could have been the first step towards a major sale. Potential opportunity..."

"Ca-ching!"

"Three point two million dollars over two years."

Richard was beside himself! He knew about this—his Director of Sales had told him only last week how much difficulty they were having in reaching the decision makers! If only he could tap Barb on the shoulder and tell her, "Talk to this guy—we need to get to know him!" He shook his head in frustration.

As the volume came back to normal, Richard realized he had moved to another table. Here he found Josh Fordyce deep in conversation with someone he vaguely recognized. "Of course!" he said to himself. "I remember this fellow—he used to be in our marketing department and moved to another company a couple of years ago." The two were strolling down Memory Lane, catching up with news.

Again the volume faded, again Brucie appeared.

"Richard, your company has been actively pursuing a contract with a construction engineering firm with global operations." Richard nodded. "Yes," he said, "that's Mopal Engineering."

"Negotiations have been tricky," continued Brucie, "and your top sales people feel that to close the deal they need to speak with one particular senior partner of Mopal. So far, they haven't been able to make contact."

Richard knew all this, and now he had a sinking feeling he knew where Brucie was leading.

"See that woman in the green suit opposite Josh? She's the wife of Mopal's senior partner. Of course, there's no guarantee that getting to know her would get you any closer to her husband, but don't you think it's worth a try for a contract potentially worth...."

"Ca-ching!"

"Five million dollars?"

Annie twirled her feather duster and whisked them both back to Richard's office.

"Richard, as I told you earlier, tonight's message is a

little different. I can't really say you specifically lost money because of these incidents, but they do represent lost opportunities with possibly large payoffs in the future.

"Besides the two people Brucie pointed out to you, there were also five others in that room that could have been entry points into companies who could do business with you. But you'll never know who they are, because your people didn't know how to exploit the opportunities."

Richard rubbed his chin thoughtfully. "I do see what you mean, Annie. I guess we had looked at these 'junkets' just from one angle, and never noticed the opportunity they offered. Maybe we should look at who holds all the memberships, event tickets, etc. from this new viewpoint."

"Most people in business have heard about networking, Richard, and some folks do it very well. But it seems as if we expect people to do it naturally, and that's unrealistic. Young people in particular often find it difficult to mingle with strangers in a setting like the awards banquet, so they need some guidance. Once again, it comes back to training."

"Yes, I do see that, Annie. We need to get them all together, explain to them the real value of networking at these events and then show them how to do it."

"Richard, I think you've got it! Now what about that slashed training budget....?"

And she was gone.

Friday night

Knowing this was the last lesson Annie was to teach him, Richard welcomed her effusively. Who could have predicted a week ago that he would be eagerly awaiting visits from this amazing woman carrying bucket, mop and magical feather duster, whose unassuming appearance masked an astounding power?

"Well Richard," said Annie, "you have a lot to think about already. Are you prepared for what you might learn in your last lesson?"

Something in Annie's tone warned Richard that he might find this lesson especially difficult, but he knew he had to learn it anyway. "Sure am, Annie. Let's go!"

The screensaver faded into another scene. This time, it was a small team meeting conducted by Paula Campbell, Manager of Direct Marketing. Annie touched the screen with her duster and with the familiar loud buzzing and flash of light, they were drawn into the computer—and into the meeting room.

Around the table sat all six members of the team: Don Ellison, Barbara Truro, Elizabeth Thornton, Cyril Kennedy, Catherine Hyde and Peter McKenna. Paula was speaking.

"The small-business mailing we did last month hasn't done as well as we hoped," she said. "I'd like to get your ideas on where we go from here. Can we salvage the campaign with a follow-up mailing, or we do need to start over with a new approach? Cyril, would you start us off?"

With a small shake of his head, Cyril shrugged. "Well, we did the mailing exactly as we decided at our planning meeting. What more could we have done?" His tone and expression made it clear that he took no share in responsibility for the setback, and he offered no further comment.

"What do you think, Catherine?" asked Paula. Catherine leaned forward and looked round the group before speaking.

"I don't know about the rest of you," she began, "but I'm not ready to write this baby off yet. We spent a lot of time on the plans, and we *all* had lots of opportunity for input." With this last comment, she looked meaningfully at Cyril. "I wonder whether the problem lies in the promotional letter—or is it perhaps in the list we used?"

"You know, I did wonder about that list," Barbara said in her thoughtful way. "It seemed like the best available, but perhaps we should have tested more small segments before rolling out the whole thing."

"Well, it's a bit late to be thinking of that now!" said Cyril, adding in a mutter, "Maybe we need some more forward-thinking leadership around here."

"Thank you for sharing *that* little piece of wisdom, Cyril" rejoined Barbara sarcastically, "but we should concentrate on constructive ideas—if you don't mind!" Cyril looking down morosely at the table, shaking his head.

Paula picked up on Barbara's first comment. "Is there a practical way to test just a segment with a follow-up letter? Maybe even two different follow-up letters to two segments? Elizabeth—lists are your domain. Can we do that?"

As Elizabeth began to speak, the sound muted and Richard felt a jolt inside his head that made him squeeze his eyes shut. When he opened them a moment later, the clock told him an hour had passed and the meeting had finished. On his way out the door, Cyril angrily complained to Don and Peter. "What kind of manager is she anyway? That's what I'd like to know. She's always asking us what to do—aren't managers supposed to be leaders?" Don appeared to agree, but Peter hurriedly moved off, escaping the discussion.

Last to leave the room, Paula was frustrated. In a way typical of the unreality of this whole amazing week, Richard found he could hear what she was thinking—and her thoughts disturbed him. "This just isn't working. I don't know whether Cyril's problem is with me personally, or just women in general. But something has to change, and soon!"

Richard noticed that the computer at the side of the room was still switched on, and the picture on the monitor was behaving strangely. Suddenly, whoosh! An irresistible force drew him towards, and into, the screen, and with the usual sound and light effects, he and Annie had changed location again.

"Wait a minute, Annie," exclaimed Richard. "Where's Brucie? Isn't this where he chimes in and tells me the cost of....something? I'm not sure I see any monetary cost here—I was waiting for him to explain."

"Oh, don't worry Richard. He's here—he'll show up when it's his moment! For now, let's listen in on the action here."

In one of the ultra-modern office pods in the Software Development Department, manager Hannah Williams was having a 'discussion' with Jennifer Benson, one of her junior programmers. Clearly, neither was happy.

"But I just don't get it. *Why* do you want me to do it this way? It doesn't make any sense," complained Jennifer.

"That's your problem, Jennifer," Hannah answered angrily. "You think that just because your brilliant mind

doesn't understand it, it must be stupid. Well, guess what—
other people have brains around here too. You may think
anyone over thirty is ignorant, but we've been around a while
and learned a few things along the way—and you're still wet
behind the ears! This is the way I want it done, so please just
do it and stop complaining! When you've been here as long as
I have, you can decide how things are done!' And with that,
she stalked away.

"Oh man!" muttered Jennifer, viciously punching her
keyboard. "No way I'm sticking around here and putting up
with idiots like her! It wouldn't be so bad if she even
understood how the technology works, but she doesn't get that
either. She probably can't even program her VCR!" Jennifer's
neighbour, Sam, snickered in agreement as they both went
back to work at their computers.

As Richard wondered who hired these know-it-all kids,
he saw Annie raise her duster towards a computer. She looked
hard at Richard and seemed to hesitate, but then went ahead

and touched the screen. In a flash, Richard found himself back in his office, and at first thought Annie was ready for their usual debriefing session.

But all at once he felt something wasn't quite as usual, and he soon had proof of that. The door opened, and in walked... Richard!

"What the...!" exclaimed Richard, jumping to his feet. "Don't worry," said Annie, gesturing him back into his seat, "it's just a scene like all the others. Let's move over to the guest chairs, where we can watch and listen."

His heart beating fast from the shock, Richard did as she said. The clock showed it was the beginning of the day, and he watched as his other self sat at the desk and began to work. The intercom buzzed, and the voice of his assistant, Maria, filled the room. "Marius is here to see you. Shall I send him in?"

Now he recognized the scene that had taken place yesterday morning, and he remembered that he hadn't really wanted to talk to Marius Grant. His Director of Finance was an excellent man, in whom he had great confidence. But his style was ponderous, and a discussion with him could be an exercise in patience. Still, he'd better see what he wanted, and asked Maria to send him in.

"Morning, Marius! How are you today?"

"Well Richard, I would like to respond traditionally and say I'm fine. But the truth is, I'm not. I am deeply concerned about the budgetary process around the new product launch. In the precarious financial situation in which we now find ourselves, it seems to me...."

Just as he had when this conversation took place, Richard now felt his eyes glaze over and his attention begin to wander. Marius' voice droned on, but the words went over Richard's head. Suddenly he realized Marius had asked him a question.

"I'm sorry Marius, could you say that last bit again for me? I was thinking about something you said earlier."

With a deep sigh and a tightening of the lips, Marius did so. In his role as observer, Richard could now see that Marius had cause to be offended by this cavalier treatment. The discussion continued for a few more minutes, and then the sound faded. The hands on the clock moved rapidly and showed that a half hour had passed, and Marius was leaving the office, head down, looking displeased.

Instantly, a subtle change in the atmosphere told Richard he was back in real time, still in his office. Before he had a chance to say a word to Annie, there was a rush of wind and a loud "Ca-ching!", and Brucie materialized in the other guest chair—complete with cash register.

"I wondered where you were tonight," said Richard

with a rueful grin. "I can't imagine what you have to show me, but I have a feeling I won't like it."

"Probably not," replied Brucie, "but if you didn't need to hear this we wouldn't be here, would we?" He went on to deliver Richard a shattering blow in a matter-of-fact tone.

"Of the people you saw in all three vignettes tonight, five are actively making plans to leave the company."

Richard gasped. This was the last thing he expected. He knew *he* had no plans to leave, so from the last scene that left Marius. Marius couldn't leave! Marius needed to be at the helm of Finance, particularly during this difficult time! "But why?" he asked desperately.

"Don't ask me—that's Annie's department. She'll tell you when I've finished."

"Who else is leaving?" cried Richard, panic-stricken.

"Paula Campbell, Peter McKenna, Hannah Williams,

Jennifer Ritchie," intoned Brucie. Ignoring Richard's indrawn breath, he continued.

"As you know, it costs a great deal of money to lose and replace people, particularly at the higher levels. There are costs associated with the person leaving, and then the search for a replacement, hiring and training can be extremely expensive. If we total up the costs you will incur when these five people leave, it comes to..."

Once again, Brucie's right ear bowed low as the cash register jumped to attention with its loud "Ca-ching!"

"...one point eight million dollars!" And both Brucie and cash register vanished.

"But Annie, why?" Richard cried again. "Why are these people leaving out of the blue?"

"Well it's not exactly 'out of the blue' Richard. Discontent has been simmering in them for some time and, just as with all the other lessons you have learned, this is about communication."

"What do you mean?" he demanded.

"Well let's start with the folks in the Direct Marketing Department. The main problem here is the ongoing conflict between Paula and Cyril, and that problem stems from one being male and the other female. Men and women communicate in vastly different styles, which results in this type of conflict more often than you realize.

"Paula's management style is—quite naturally— female. That means she asks her team members for as much input as they can give, so that she can mull it all over and use it to come up with what she considers the best decisions. Nothing wrong with that—it works well for her. The problem is that many men—in this case Cyril—mistake this style for weakness. When she asks for input, Cyril thinks she is asking what she should do, and he therefore feels contempt for her.

Paula wants to work in a less stressful environment, so she is working on her resume.

"Peter is simply so fed up with the wrangling and constant stress that he just wants out of the situation, so he is leaving too."

Richard's expression of panic gradually changed to interest, as this new aspect of communication sank in. "But what can we do?"

"This is just one example of the problems between the men and women in your company, and there are many more. Enlightened organizations are taking steps to educate and sensitize their employees to male/female style differences, because you can see what's at stake here. Perhaps you should think about this."

"OK. Now what about Hannah and—what was her name?..Jennifer? I could see problems there and my first instinct was to blame Jennifer."

"That's because you are closer in age to Hannah, Richard. Your philosophy of management has developed over the whole length of your career, and it has served you so well that you haven't questioned it. But take a look at your workforce. This is not a homogenous group, but a blend of three different generations—why should you be surprised there are communication issues? Particularly in industries like yours, the knowledge work is more and more in the hands of young people not far into their careers. Although they are new to the company, they have advanced knowledge of the technologies they use in their work. Because many of those who manage them are not so adept in technology, the younger workers don't respect them as much as you may think they should.

"On the other side of the picture, the older managers hold the view that you do as you are told, and you must 'pay your dues' through length of service before you have influence over the work.

"You have some excellent people in your company, Richard, including Hannah and Jennifer and others of all ages. But their apparent inability to get along and work productively together creates a tension that some find too much to handle— and they see moving on as the only solution."

"It's true, Annie. My counterparts in other organizations often complain about the work ethic and attitude of younger workers, but you've made me see that there are problems on both sides. I suppose you're going to tell me it's training again," he said, grinning at Annie.

"You've got it, Richard!"

But Richard's grin disappeared as he remembered what happened in his own office just yesterday. "But what about Marius? Why is *he* leaving?"

"Many companies conduct exit interviews when employees leave—as you do. Studies of these interviews have shown time and again that people leave because they don't feel they are listened to—and therefore they don't feel valued. Even if they don't articulate it exactly that way, they often complain that there's no communication in the company.

"You've said how highly you esteem Marius, so you may be surprised to learn that he doesn't believe that at all. Marius feels his opinions are not valued and that you don't have much time for him. He is frustrated, and wants to find a company that will appreciate him."

"But that's ridiculous, Annie. How could he think I don't appreciate him?"

Annie didn't answer, instead leaving Richard to mull over the scene in his office the day before.

"I do see, yes," he said finally. "It's communication again. I really didn't give him much attention this morning. I wonder if I am offending others this way too. How can I undo the damage?"

"Richard, you can keep all five of these people. It's not too late to make them change their minds, but it will take some very effective communication on your part. But I know you can do it," she smiled.

"Well, Annie, you promised me a lesson every night this week, and you've certainly given me more food for thought than I ever expected. So where do I go from here?"

"Communication is The Hidden Profit Center, Richard. It's hidden because most people think of it as a 'soft skill' and don't consider it as a way to improve the financial aspect of business. And it's a profit centre because good communication can save so much unnecessary expense that it automatically benefits the bottom line.

"As you said yourself, laying people off is at best a temporary, one-shot solution. But continuous improvement in communication can pay dividends well into the future."

"Yes, I can see that now," said Richard, nodding thoughtfully.

"Here are three common myths that get in the way of success:

1. *Communication is a 'soft skill'*. No, it's a set of skills with a direct effect on profitability.

2. *Communication skills come naturally to people*. No they don't. You've got to train them.

3. *One communication training program suits everyone in the company*. No it doesn't. To uncover and benefit from The Hidden Profit Center, you need a specific type of training. People *first* have to understand how their communication affects profitability, and *only then* can they learn to develop their skills effectively.

"Richard, next week you have to make some serious decisions about your company's future. You have the weekend to think about all this. I have confidence in you, and I know you will come up with the right answers."

"Does this mean you're leaving me on my own now?"

"For now," smiled Annie. "You don't need me any more, but I'll be watching how everything works out. Perhaps I'll visit you again so that you can share your success with me!"

And once again, Annie gathered up her bucket, mop and feather duster. As she opened the door, she looked over her shoulder at Richard and smiled—and was gone.

Monday morning

Richard paced the floor in front of his desk. Full of nervous energy, he could hardly contain himself, as he waited for Maria's call. Finally, it came. All the members of Richard's executive group were available for the meeting he had just called. They would be in the boardroom at 10 a.m. sharp.

For Richard, the past weekend had been like no other. His weekends were usually spent with his family, but he had asked them for their patience over the next two days. He explained that the upcoming week would be hugely important for the company, and that for this one weekend he would like them to carry on without him as he spent the time in his study. Sophie and the girls had agreed, pursuing their own activities without him, just this once.

He spent long hours reliving a variety of events and situations in the life of his company, paying attention to the communication issues in the light of Annie's lessons—and imagining what Brucie and his cash register would have to say about them! No question—much Hidden Profit Center training was needed.

Next, he applied himself to the practical. How much of The Hidden Profit Center could be accessed in the short term? He needed fast results if he were to avoid layoffs and still keep the company profitable. Just based on the examples Annie had shown him, he identified a number of areas of need and the training that could bring dramatic change. Oh yes, the long hours of Saturday and Sunday had challenged his intellect, his emotions, his mental stamina and his drive.

At the executive meeting this morning, he would need to muster all his powers of communication, of persuasion, to sell his top people on his plan. Then he would need strength and determination to guide them through its implementation. He felt up to the challenge. "Bring 'em on, Annie!" he whispered to the empty office.

Just before ten, they began to arrive. As they took their seats, they looked apprehensively at Richard, obviously expecting gloomy news.

"Well ladies and gentlemen," he began with a confident smile for everyone in the group, "today is the beginning of a new era for this company. We have an opportunity to make this great organization even greater, and together we're going to take that opportunity!"

The somber expressions changed to puzzlement, and then to surprised interest as he continued.

"First, there will be no layoffs. The people in our factories and offices are the best—that's why we hired them. They helped the company reach the profit levels of recent years, and I won't dump them now at the first sign of trouble.

"Second, the training budget is not only reinstated, but doubled. We will revisit it in six months to see if it needs to be increased."

A murmur of surprise went around the table. They had agonized over where to cut expenses, finally deciding the training budget was expendable, and here was Richard putting it back. How would that help? But he certainly had their attention.

"There's a huge, widespread problem in this company, and that's the terrible state of communication. I've come to realize it is costing us a great deal of money, and if we can first quantify the costs and then correct the problem, we can find a Hidden Profit Center right here.

"So, instead of awarding training contracts on the basis of the best price, we will actively—and quickly—seek out specialists who can not only find The Hidden Profit Center in our communication, but also train our people to exploit it.

"Third, we in this room are not immune to poor communication. I'm guilty, you're guilty. We need training too, and we're going to get it."

Although he obviously couldn't reveal the unlikely source of his information, Richard enumerated the costs of the company's poor communication at all levels and in all areas, putting numbers to the potential savings to be had from improvement. His excitement and passion were palpable, and soon every man and woman in the executive group was infected and eager to be part of this great initiative.

"OK, folks," he said with confidence, "let's roll up our sleeves and get to work. We need a plan to make this happen— and fast! I want to start with a brainstorming session right now. I want completely open communication. This is hereby declared a safe zone, where each one of you may voice his or her concerns and ideas with no fear of reprisal. There is a ban on all knee-jerk negativity—all ideas and thoughts are welcome.

"By the time we leave this office today, we'll be ready, willing and able to put our plan into action—and we'll do it. Are you with me?"

Heads nodded. Sleeves were rolled up. Brains clicked into gear.

"OK—let's get started!"

Epilogue—one year later

Ten o'clock Monday night. Outside the office window, the lights of a thousand tall buildings punctuated the night sky—the stone canyons of the business district never sleep. Gazing down at a scene so familiar he hardly noticed it any more, Richard Pemberton wondered how many offices in those other buildings contained men and women doing exactly as he was doing now—preparing confidently to face their shareholders.

A soft knock at the door interrupted his thoughts, and he looked up.

"Annie!" he cried delightedly, rising and coming to meet her.

"Richard, I don't need to ask how you are! You look like a different man from the one I met a year ago."

"I feel like a different man, Annie, leading a different company! And it's all thanks to you."

Annie sat down in front of Richard's desk, smiling." So tell me all about it."

"Well you know, Annie," Richard began earnestly, "it wasn't easy, especially at first. The executive group were all on board from the beginning, and they threw themselves into the spirit of the new organization. When it came time to put it all into practice, though, there were the usual roadblocks. Employees resisted, managers saw faults in everyone else but not in themselves, stock analysts criticized us for doing nothing they could see.

"But you know, because we had a plan in place that we could all believe in, we just simply made it work. What set us off on the right track was our newfound realization of what poor communication had been costing us. We finally understood that communication is not a separate discipline. It's actually the lifeblood of the organization, and when it doesn't flow well, the whole organism is in danger. We were at that point a year ago—before I met you and Brucie!"

Annie smiled and nodded, as Richard proudly pointed to handsomely framed document on the wall.

"As you can see, Annie, we began by embedding communication as one of the core principles of our corporate value statement. And believe me, it's not just a statement on paper—we have been living this ideal for more than half a year now.

"We found the right trainers and facilitators, rallied the employees to the cause and eventually got the program rolling. I have thought of Brucie many times throughout the past year, thinking how I would love to have his trusty cash register "Ca-ching!" with the savings we have achieved through our Hidden Profit Center!

"Tomorrow I can face the board and the shareholders with pride, both in myself and my people. We have stopped the bleeding, and the recovery is well underway—and we laid off not a single employee!"

Annie smiled. "You know, Richard, I *could* use the old feather duster technique to show you tomorrow's shareholder meeting—but I won't." Seeing Richard's hopeful expression disappear, she added, "But I will tell you that you will be beaming happily at the end, and so will the shareholders, the executive, the managers and the employees!"

"I can't wait, Annie, not just for the meeting, but for

what the future holds for this company. Not only have we
realized great financial benefits by uncovering The Hidden
Profit Center, but in the process we have enlisted the co-
operation and loyalty of our people to a degree I never would
have believed. It's an exciting place to be, and I know we have
an amazing future. I can't thank you enough for what you've
done for me, and for my company."

"Now you're embarrassing me, Richard!" quipped
Annie. "I just showed you the way, and you took it. Although
you won't be able to see me, I will be keeping an eye on things
and enjoying your success. I'll never be far away, and if you
ever need me, just sit at your desk one night and ask for me."

With that she stood up. "I'm ready to leave myself,
Annie. Let's go out together." Gathering up his coat and
briefcase, he guided Annie towards the door and busied himself
switching off the lights.

Unseen by Richard, Annie looked over her shoulder

and grinned. On the desk, Richard's computer screen was suddenly filled with Brucie's face. His right ear bowed low as he tipped Annie an enormous wink—and vanished.

Finding and exploiting The Hidden Profit Center in your organization

There *is* a Hidden Profit Center in *your* organization, and the following guidelines are designed to help you find and exploit it. Some will choose to introduce the program throughout their organizations, while others will begin with a pilot in just one area. If you have control over just one department, you can put the program into action there. However you decide to implement the program, use these guidelines as a starting point, adapt them and flesh out the details as appropriate.

SETTING THE STAGE

The success or failure of any large-scale organizational plan depends on those who are expected to implement it, so you must help your people understand The Hidden Profit Center program.

- Present an organization-wide message to introduce and explain the program.
- Appoint Hidden Profit Center Circles. These are the people who will carry out the tasks needed to implement the plan. There may be several circles or just one, depending on the size of your organization and whether you begin with the whole organization or just one section. The number of people in each circle will also depend on the size of the task. Members of the circles must understand the program completely and be 100% committed to it. Each circle must contain at least one person, probably from Human Resources, who has access to confidential salary information, as this will be needed to quantify the costs of communication.
- Circles study the current state of communication, instituting Hidden Profit Center training to focus on areas of weakness.
- Announce successes to everyone in the organization, and reward them appropriately.

MEETINGS

- Survey various departments over a period of a month, compare the results with previous year if possible, and determine answers to the following:
  —How many meetings are held?
  —How long do the meetings last?
  —How many attend and at what levels?
- The Human Resources representative on the circle calculates the direct cost of attendees for each meeting.
- Circle members assess other costs—refer to Brucie's tally for the Monday meeting in the story.
- Institute appropriate training to exploit The Hidden Profit Center in meetings.
- The Circle continues to monitor meetings, measuring improvement and savings.

WRITTEN COMMUNICATION

- Be prepared for this segment to take some time.
- Designate a specific month as "Find The Hidden Profit Center in our Writing" month.
- Provide time sheets to record the time spent on writing. When recording items that need drafting, editing, redrafting, peer review, etc., *all* this time should be attributed to the item.
- The Circle representative in Human Resources assigns direct salary costs to all writing for the month. Note that this is a large task, and may require several Circle members.
- Simultaneously, writing experts (outside or in-house, depending on available expertise) examine a cross-section of writing samples, judging writing style, clarity, conciseness, effectiveness.
- Circle members contact clients and other external correspondents to gauge response to written communication, with emphasis on comprehension and appropriateness. Comments are gathered anonymously and tabulated.
- Institute appropriate training to exploit The Hidden Profit Center in written communication.
- Monitor through periodic spot checks after training is complete.

PRESENTATIONS

- Circle members interview employees and management at various levels to find out:
  — the average number and length of presentations given
  — how effective they are in the eyes of those who must listen to them.
- Find out from the listeners what presenters do well and what needs improvement.
- The Circle representative in Human Resources assigns direct salary costs to all presentations for a given length of time. This is a large task, and may require several Circle members.
- Approach selected clients to whom presentations have been made as part of the sales process. Find out how the presentation influenced the win or loss of sales and why. Comments are gathered anonymously and tabulated.
- Institute appropriate training to exploit The Hidden Profit Center in presentations.
- Circle members randomly audit presentations to assess improvements and ongoing areas of weakness.

MEMBERSHIPS, NETWORKING, BUSINESS DEVELOPMENT

- Create a matrix of everyone who is sponsored for any type of club membership, as well as special events.
- Each person should create an annual plan to meet people and cultivate relationships at events, as well as expand and exploit their network for future business.
- Provide Hidden Profit Center training in networking for all those involved in business development.
- This process should be repeated as part of each year's business planning cycle.

OTHER AREAS

- Hidden Profit Center Circles conduct interviews and surveys to uncover communication roadblocks due to gender conflicts, inter-generational challenges and multi-cultural issues.
- Sensitivity training should be provided in these areas.

- Circles should conduct ongoing monitoring of all areas in order to catch potential problems before they develop.

GENERAL

- The Hidden Profit Center program needs to be carefully announced, explained and introduced. Pockets of resistance are to be expected, and it is in the organization's interests to work through these.
- New circles should be appointed from time to time to keep the program fresh.
- At set times throughout each year, depending on rate of employee turnover, new people should be given Hidden Profit Center training in appropriate areas.
- Incentive and reward programs should be developed to help build and maintain the program and continue to achieve positive results.
- MHW Communications is available to provide Hidden Profit Center consulting and training. For an initial discussion without obligation, call 416-966-5023 or e-mail hwilkie@mhwcom.com.
- We invite you to contact Helen Wilkie to share your success stories of finding your organization's Hidden Profit Center.

Ca-ching!

Afterword by the Author

For years I have heard managers and executives discuss the importance of communication. Yet I have noticed two interesting facts:

- More often than not, they can't define what they mean by communication, and
- In designing training plans or conference programs, they think of communication as a "soft skill", with low priority.

I have long thought about writing a book to show how wrong this thinking is, but struggled to find the right vehicle. I hope I have found it in Brucie, Annie and Richard.

The lessons are deceptively simple, but the potential gains from acting on them are immense. I want to know what you have been able to achieve in your search for *your* organization's Hidden Profit Center, and I invite you to share your success stories with me. Send an e-mail to hwilkie@mhwcom.com or call me at 1-416-966-5023.

As I write this, plans are underway for the creation of a Hidden Profit Center Web site, where we will offer ongoing support and information for those involved in Hidden Profit Center programs. We also plan an electronic newsletter and other initiatives as our Hidden Profit Center community grows. Join us at http://www.HiddenProfitCenter.com.

Helen Wilkie
Toronto, 2003

For information on **Hidden Profit Center**™ keynote,
training programs and consulting, visit
www.HiddenProfitCenter.com

or contact Helen Wilkie at

MHW Communications
90 Warren Road, Suite 202
Toronto, Ontario
Canada M4V 2S2

Telephone: 1-416-966-5023
e-mail:hwilkie@mhwcom.com

**Help your people understand the power of
The Hidden Profit Center ™
by giving them each a copy of this book.
Call for information on quantity pricing for premiums,
sales promotion, fundraising or educational use.**